Concepts of Piano Theory

Level 3

Dear Teacher,

Concepts of Piano Theory provides a basic understanding of music, increases sight-reading abilities and prepares the student to analyze compositions at the earliest levels.

Each workbook introduces new terms and concepts that are reinforced with worksheets, practice exercises and composition analysis. Concepts learned in earlier levels are reviewed, tested and expanded upon in advancing levels. Answers to the **Level 3** tests, worksheets and exercises may be found in the **Concepts of Piano Theory, Teacher's Key**.

This workbook is made from recycled paper. By using products that are made from recycled materials, you are helping reduce landfills and recover renewable resources.

For a complete understanding of music, a thorough study of theory is necessary. **Concepts of Piano Theory** provides the information that should be understood by every advancing pianist.

Copyright © by ReSa Publications, P. O. Box 432, Livermore, CA 94551. All rights reserved.
WARNING: The music, text, design and graphics in this publication are protected by copyright law.
It is unlawful to copy or reproduce any part of this workbook.   A466444
Printed in U.S.A. on 50% recycled paper, using Soy Ink.

TABLE OF CONTENTS

Level 3   Page

Composition Analysis	1
Accidentals	5
Worksheet	6
Major Scales	7
Major, minor, Augmented and diminished Triads	8
Perfect and Major Intervals	9
Worksheet	10
Five-Finger Patterns and Triads	11
Minor Scales	12
Composition Analysis	14
Major Key Signatures	16
Primary and Secondary Triads	19
Inversions of the Triad	21
Worksheet	22
Dynamics and Terms	23
Composition Analysis	24
Review Test	26
Composers	28
Composition Analysis	30
Rhythm and Meter	32
Worksheet	33
Composition Analysis	34
Test	35

Sonatine

Questions for this composition are on pages 3 and 4.

Muzio Clementi, Op. 36 Nr. 6

REVIEW TEST

Find the answers to the following questions from the **excerpt of the composition** on pages 1 and 2.

1. Name the Key Signature. _____

2. What is the meter? _____

3. Write the letter-names of the half-step in measure pre 1. _____ _____

4. How many beats are there in each measure? _____

5. What beat does the composition start on ? _____

6. Write the time values of the notes found in measure 1. _____ _____

7. How many Sixteenth-notes are there in measure 2? _____

8. What is the time value of the rests found in measure 3? _____

9. Name the Major Five-Finger Pattern in measure 4. _____

10. Are there any triplets in this composition? _____

11. Name the Harmonic interval in the Bass Clef in measure 7. _____

12. Name the minor Five-Finger Pattern in measure 9. _____

13. Name the Major Scale found in measure 10. _____

14. Name the minor Five-Finger Patterns in measure 11. _____ _____

15. Name the accidental in measure 12. _____

16. Name the accidental in measure 13. _____

17. Write the letter-names of the half-step and the **whole step in measure 14**.

    ____ ____   ____ ____
    Half-Step   Whole Step

18. Write the letter-names of ledger line and space notes ABOVE the Treble Clef in measure 15.

    ____ ____ ____

19. Name the Harmonic interval in measure 16. _____

20. Name the Major Scale in measure 20. _____

21. What is the time value of the rest in the Bass Clef in measure 18? _____

22. Name the Major Triad in measure 22. _____

23. How many Eighth-notes are in measure 22? _____

24. What is the time value of the rest in measure 22? _____

25. Name the Harmonic intervals in the Bass Clef in measure 30.

    _____   _____   _____

26. Name the Major and minor Five-Finger Patterns found in measure 32.

    _____   _____
            Major   minor

27. Name the Major Five-Finger Patterns in measure 33.

    _____   _____

28. Should this composition be played slowly or quickly? _____

29. In what period of music history was this composition written? _____

30. Write the letter-names of the Authentic Cadence in measures 37 and 38.

    ___ ___ ___   ___ ___ ___
         V   I

    What is the key of the cadence? _____

    Is it the same as the Key Signature? _____

ACCIDENTALS

There are <u>five</u> signs used in writing music to raise or lower tones that are not found in the Key Signature. Three of these (Sharp ♯ , Flat ♭ , and Natural ♮) move the tone one half-step up or down.

The other two used are: ♭♭ Double Flat -- which <u>lowers</u> the tone a <u>whole</u> step.

                             ✗ Double Sharp -- which <u>raises</u> the tone a <u>whole</u> step.

Remember accidentals continue to raise or lower a tone for one measure.

EXAMPLES:

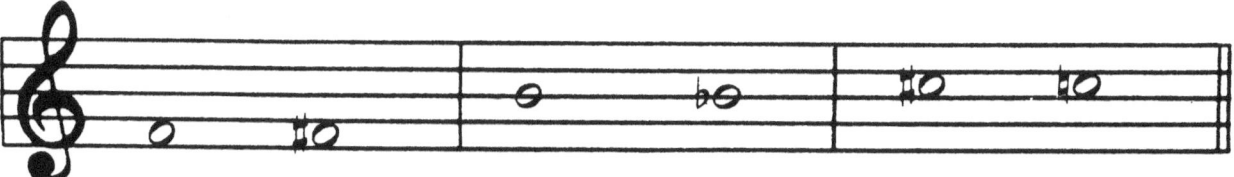

raised one half-step   lowered one half-step   lowered one half-step

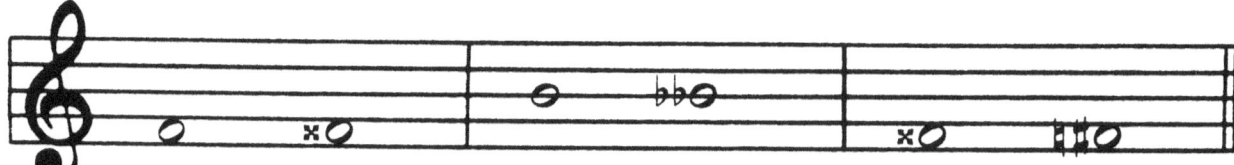

raised one whole step   lowered one whole step   lowered one half-step

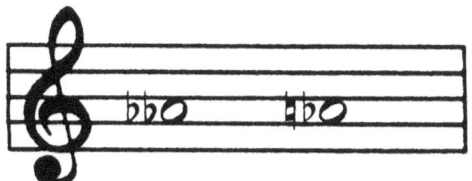

raised one half-step

WORKSHEET

1. Using accidentals <u>raise</u> each note one half-step.
   DO NOT CHANGE LETTER-NAME.

2. Using accidentals <u>lower</u> each note one half-step.
   DO NOT CHANGE LETTER-NAME.

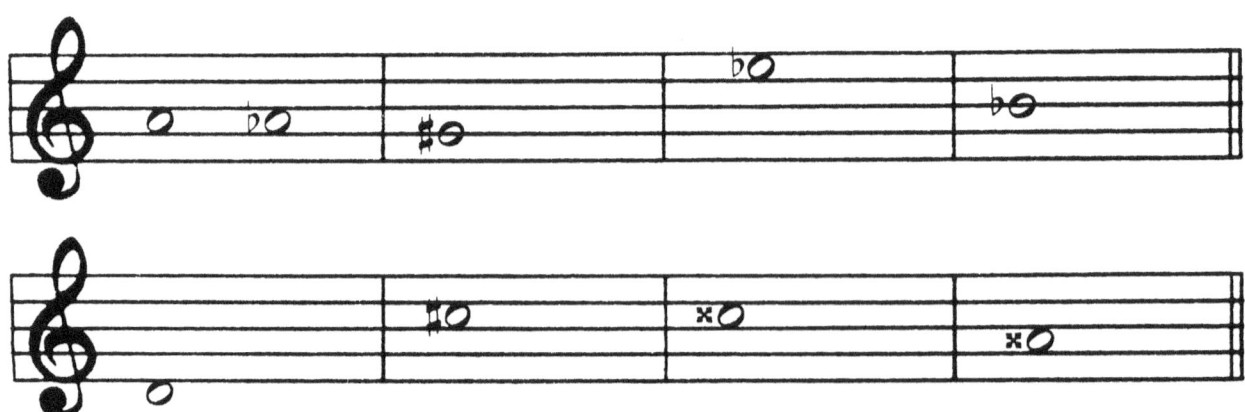

3. Using accidentals <u>raise</u> each note one whole step.
   DO NOT CHANGE LETTER-NAME.

4. Using accidentals <u>lower</u> each note one whole step.
   DO NOT CHANGE LETTER-NAME.

MAJOR SCALES

Using the whole step, half-step pattern (W-W-H-W-W-W-H) draw Major Scales one octave from key-tones below. Use accidentals. Mark half-steps with slurs.

REMEMBER: The accidental must be placed on the same line or space as the note. A sharp raises a tone a half-step and a flat lowers a tone a half-step.

MAJOR, MINOR, AUGMENTED AND DIMINISHED TRIADS

Draw Major, minor, Augmented, and diminished Triads on the notes below.

REMEMBER: The Major Triad is formed from the 1st, 3rd, and 5th degrees of the Five-Finger Pattern or diatonic scale.

Major Triads become minor by lowering the 3rd degree one half-step.
Major Triads become Augmented by raising the 5th degree one half-step.
Major Triads become diminished by lowering the 3rd and 5th degrees one half-step.

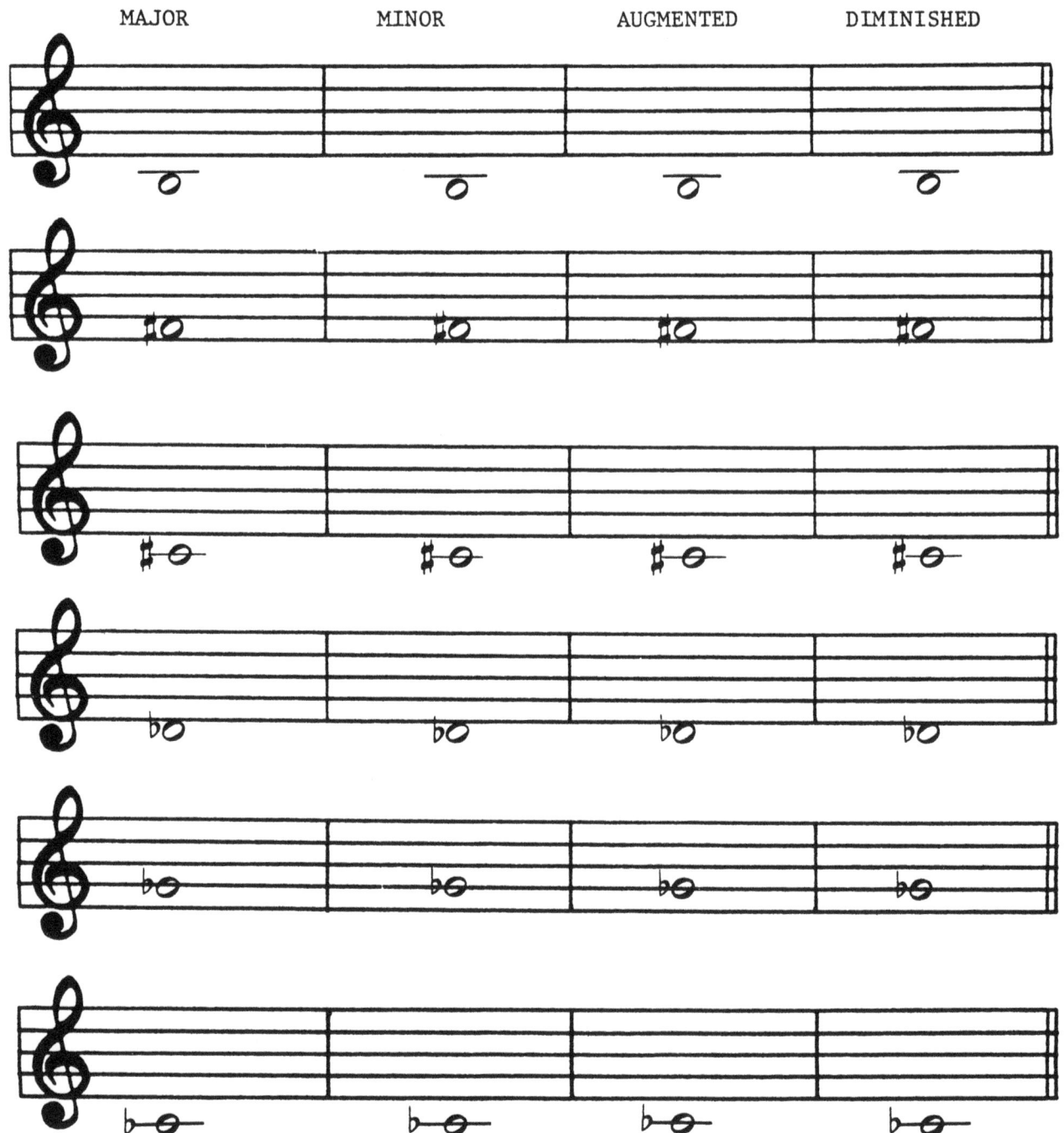

PERFECT AND MAJOR INTERVALS

In drawing intervals from tones of any Major Scale the 1st, 4th, 5th, and 8th (octave) are called <u>PERFECT</u>; all others are <u>MAJOR</u>

EXAMPLE:

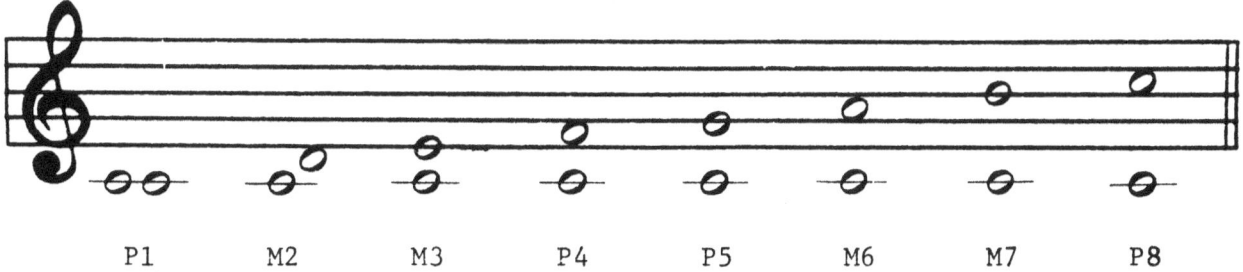

P1 M2 M3 P4 P5 M6 M7 P8

Perfect and Major intervals can also be found by counting the half-steps. There are 12 half-steps in each octave.

Perfect 1st (Prime)	No half-steps
Major 2nd	2 half-steps
Major 3rd	4 half-steps
Perfect 4th	5 half-steps
Perfect 5th	7 half-steps
Major 6th	9 half-steps
Major 7th	11 half-steps
Perfect 8th (octave)	12 half-steps

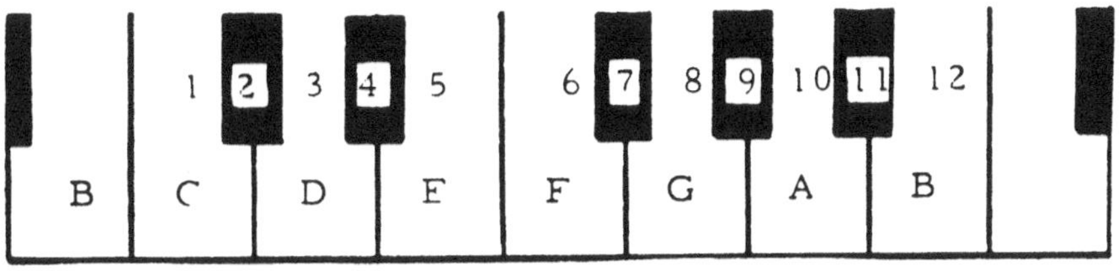

Copyright A46644 by ReSa Publications
CPT 3

WORKSHEET

1. Draw Perfect intervals from notes below. Use accidentals.

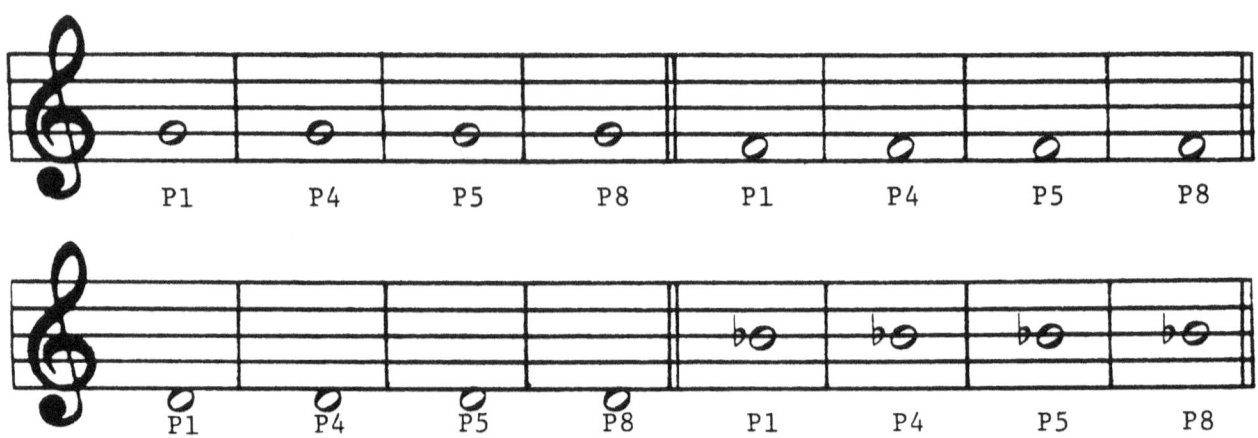

2. Draw Major intervals from notes below. Use accidentals.

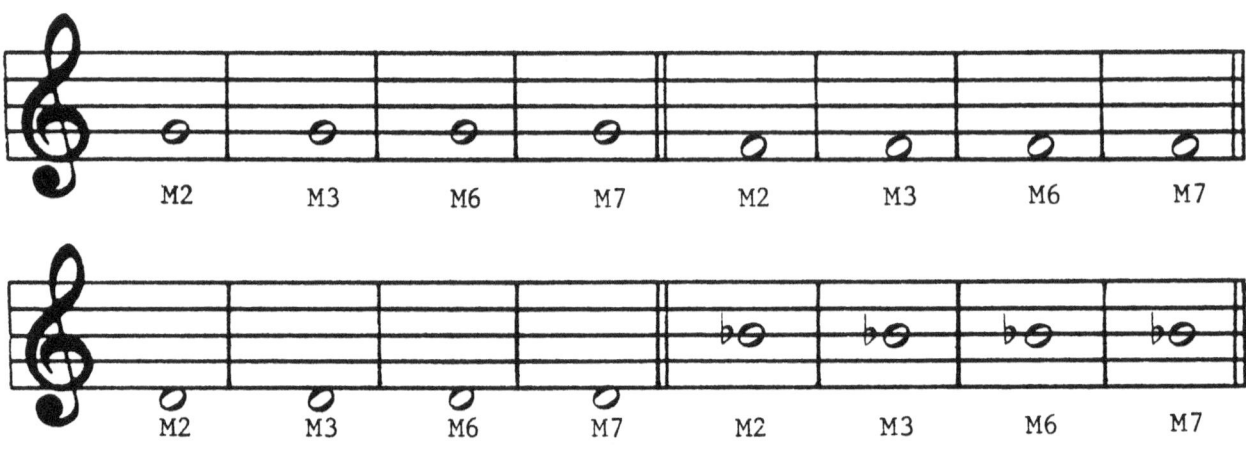

3. Draw intervals of these Major Scales. Use accidentals. Label

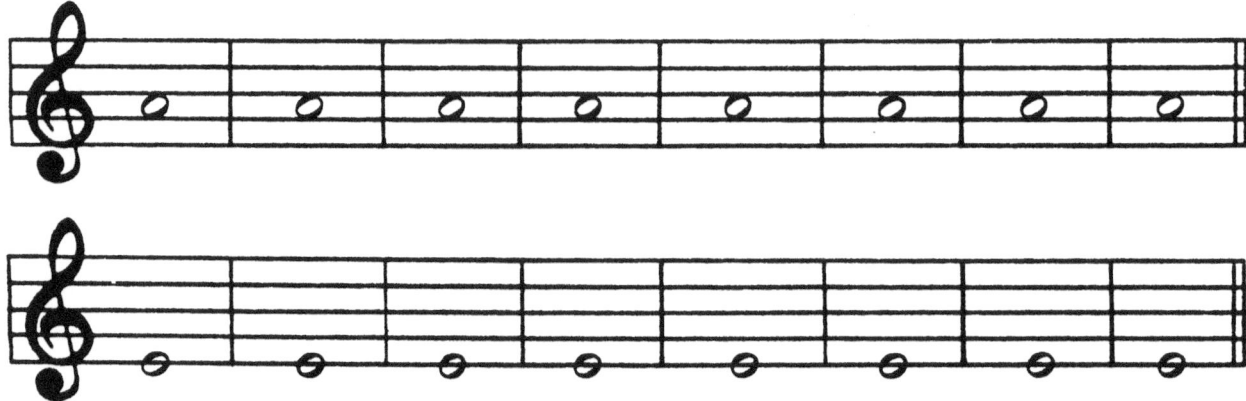

FIVE-FINGER PATTERNS AND TRIADS

1. Draw five-finger patterns from notes below.

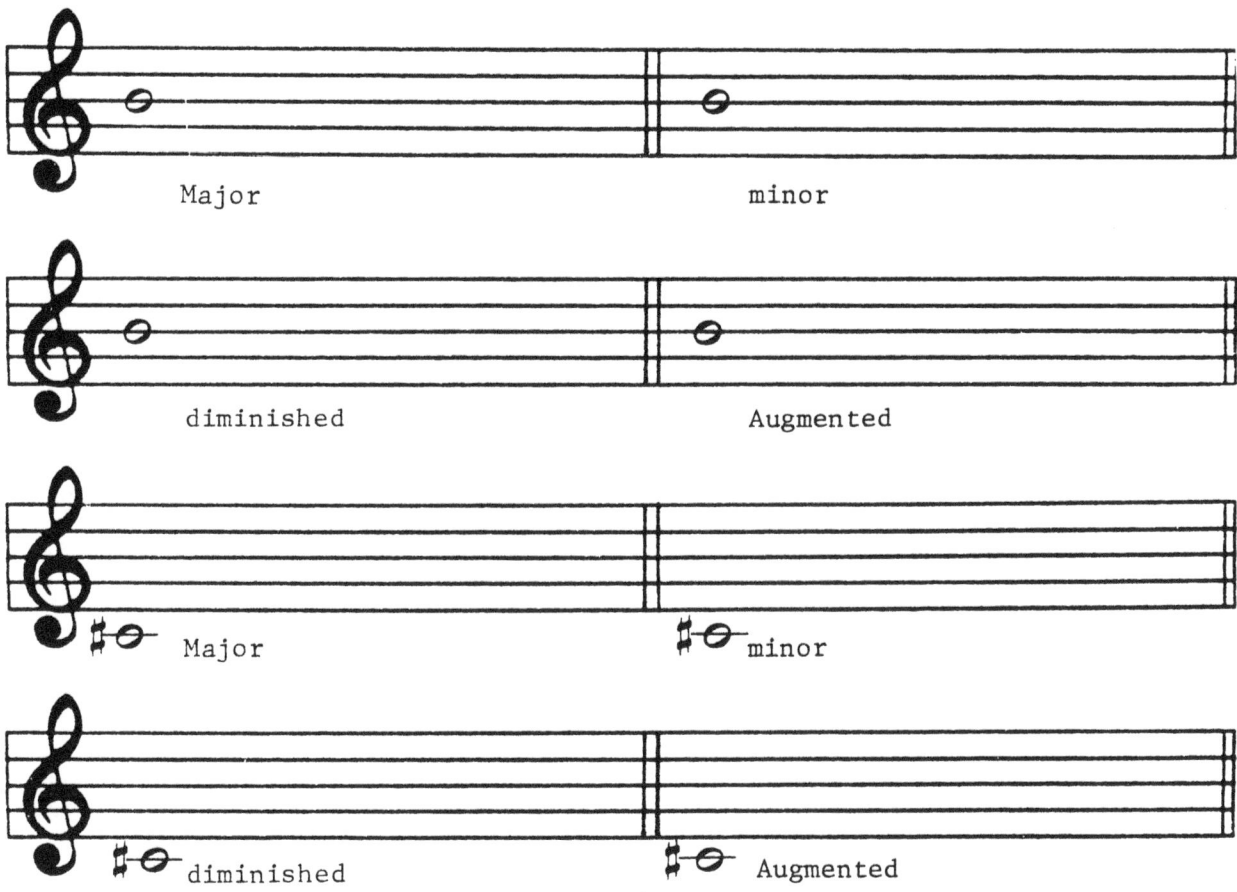

2. Draw triads from notes below. (M = Major, m = minor, d = diminished, and A = Augmented)

MINOR SCALES

Major and minor Scales are formed by the use of the seven letters of the music alphabet.

The difference between the Major and minor Scales is in the arrangements of the whole steps and half-steps.

The <u>MINOR SCALE</u> in its <u>NATURAL FORM</u> has half-steps between degrees <u>2 and 3</u>, and <u>5 and 6</u>.

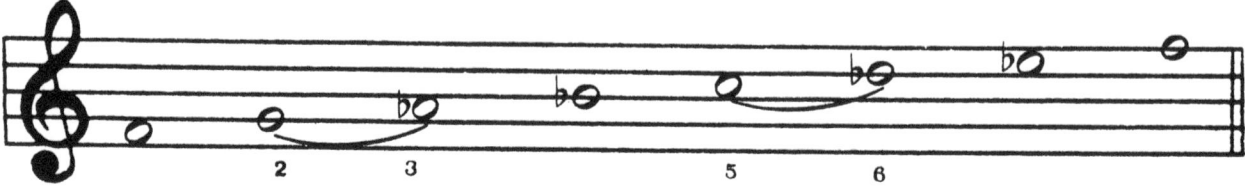

The <u>HARMONIC MINOR SCALE</u> differs from the Natural minor because the 7th degree of the scale is raised one half-step. By raising the 7th degree, there are <u>three</u> half-steps between degrees <u>6 and 7</u>. The half-steps are between degrees <u>2 and 3</u>, <u>5 and 6</u>, and <u>7 and 8</u>.

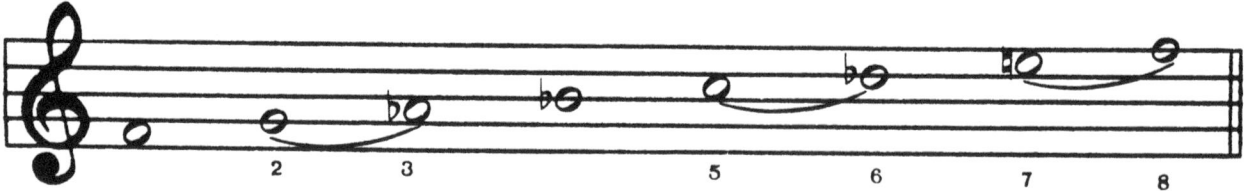

The <u>MELODIC MINOR SCALE</u> when ascending has both the 6th and 7th degrees raised; and when descending it is like the Natural minor Scale. The half-steps are between degrees <u>2 and 3</u>, and <u>7 and 8</u>.

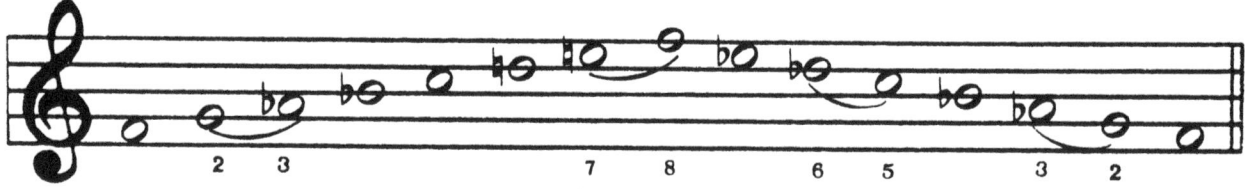

1. Draw the Natural minor Scale one octave from notes below.

1. (continued)

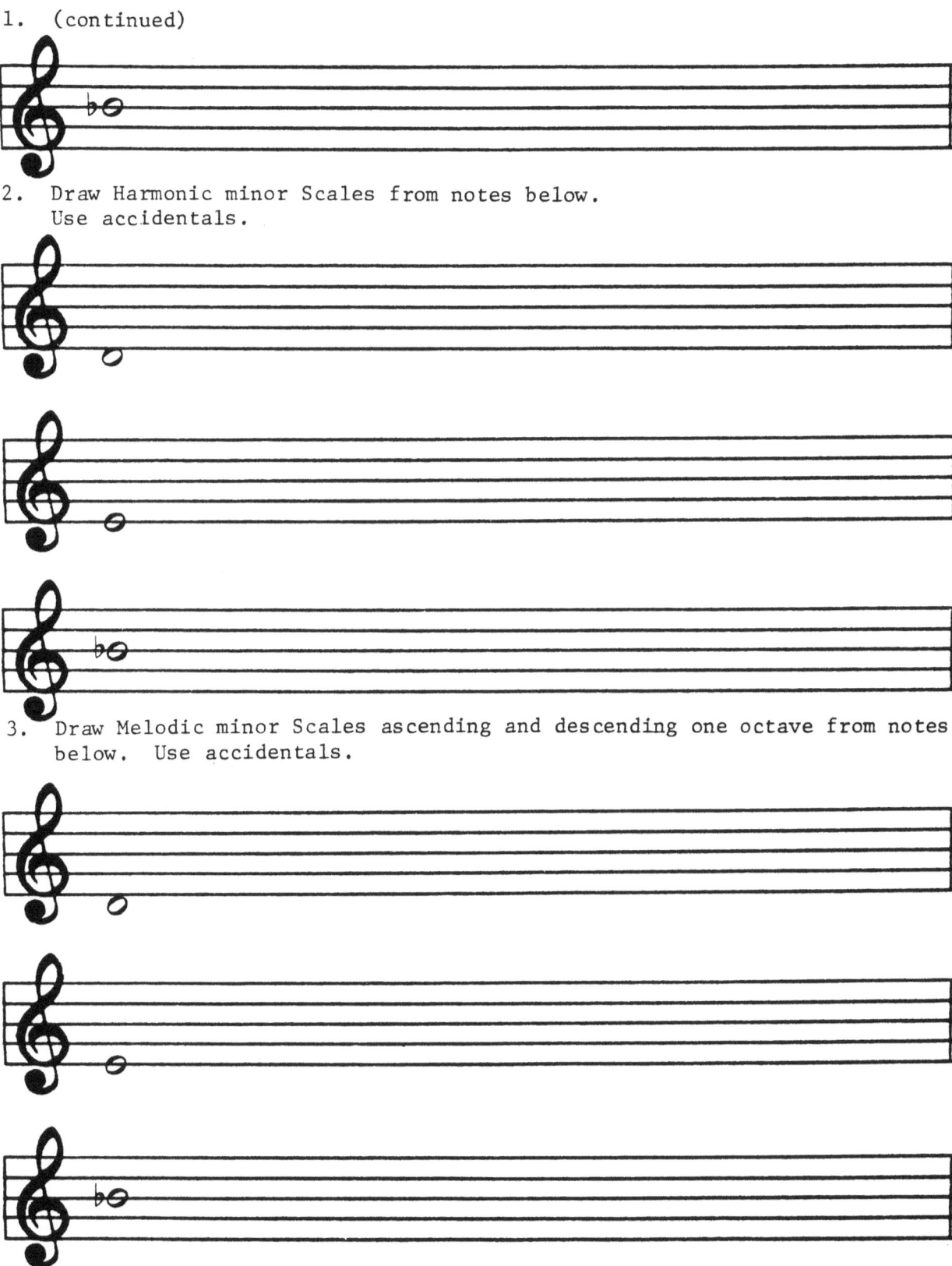

2. Draw Harmonic minor Scales from notes below. Use accidentals.

3. Draw Melodic minor Scales ascending and descending one octave from notes below. Use accidentals.

Use the BASS CLEF Sign and copy each of the scales on pages 12 and 13 on manuscript paper. Add these pages to your notebook.

Copyright A46644 by ReSa Publications
CPT 3

Allegretto.

COMPOSITION ANALYSIS

Find the answers to the following questions in the composition on page 14.

1. Name the Harmonic interval in measure 4. _____
2. Is it a Major or minor interval? _____
3. Write the letter-names of the half-step in measure 8. _____ _____
4. Name the five-finger pattern in measure 11. _____
5. Is the pattern Major or minor? _____
6. Name the five-finger pattern in measure 12. _____
7. Is the pattern Major or minor? _____
8. What is the time value of the rest in measure 16? _____
9. Name the accidentals in measure 20. _____ _____
10. Name the accidental in measure 21. _____
11. Name the broken triad in measure 22. _____
12. Is the triad Major or minor? _____
13. Name the Harmonic interval in measure 23. _____
14. Write the letter-names of the half-step in measure 24. _____ _____
15. Name the Harmonic intervals in measure 28. _____ _____
16. Name the Harmonic intervals in measure 30. _____ _____
17. Name the Harmonic triad in measure 31. _____
18. Is the triad in 1st inversion or 2nd inversion? _____
19. Is the cadence between measures 30 - 31 a Plagal or an Authentic Cadence? _____
20. In what key is the composition written? _____

MAJOR KEY SIGNATURES

The following patterns show where the sharps and flats are placed on the Grand Staff.

From F#, down four staff degrees, up five, down four, down four more, up five, and down four.

From B♭, up four staff degrees and down five degrees. This pattern continues until F♭ is reached.

1. Draw a Major Scale, followed by the Key Signature for that scale, from each tone below.

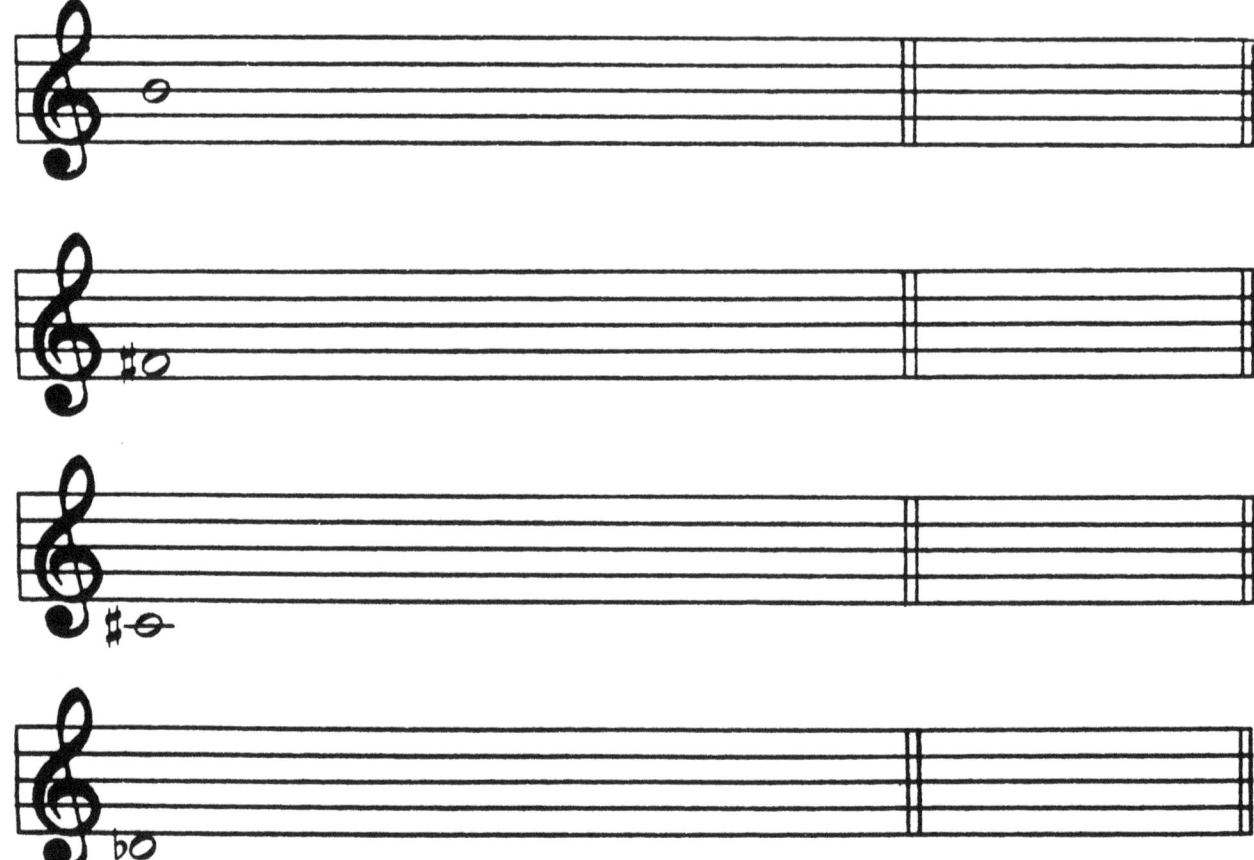

1. (continued)

2. Name the following Major Key Signatures.
   NOTE: Key Signatures may be recognized in relationship to the scale or
   by using one of the following rules.
   1) In any sharp Key Signature, a HALF-STEP above the last sharp names the key.

   2) In any flat Key Signature, the second to last flat names the key.

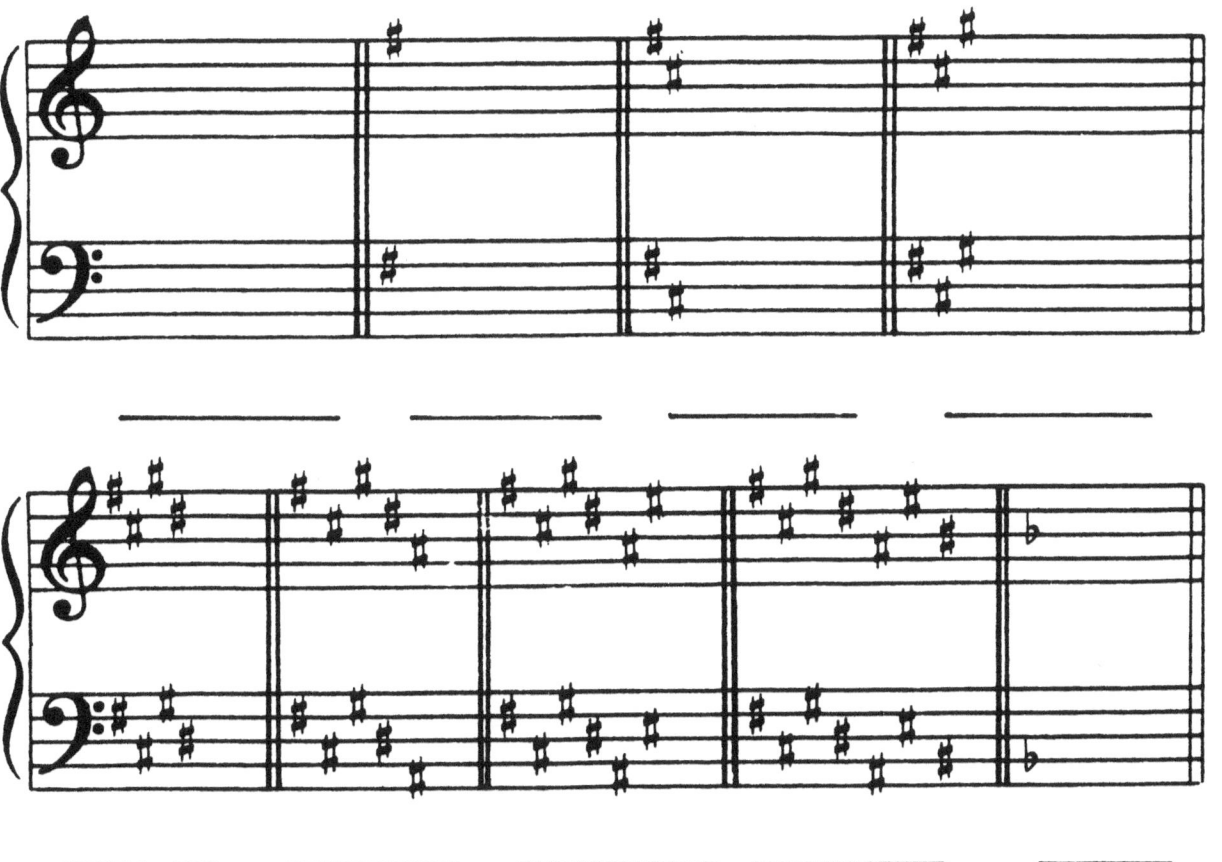

2. (continued)

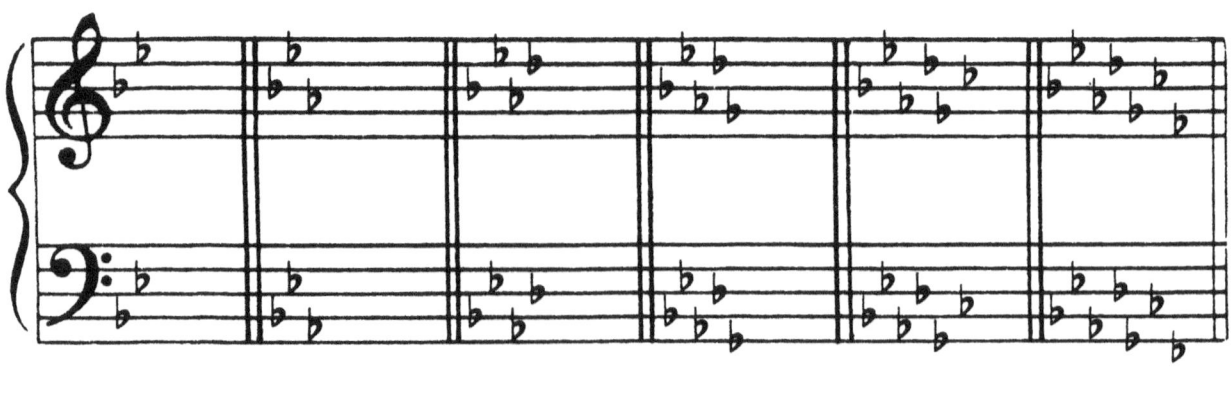

3. Draw Perfect and Major intervals in the key of G. Use accidentals. Label.

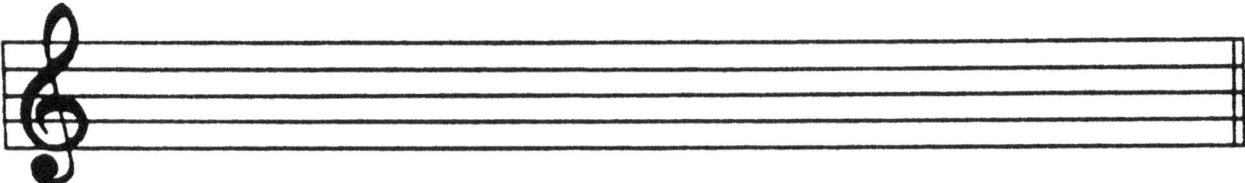

4. Draw Perfect and Major intervals in the key of F. Use accidentals. Label.

5. Draw Perfect and Major intervals in the key of D. Use accidentals. Label.

6. Draw Perfect and Major intervals in the key of B flat. Use accidentals. Label.

PRIMARY AND SECONDARY TRIADS

Triads can be made from any tone of a scale. In a Major Scale the triads made from the first, fourth, and fifth tones are the most important. They are called PRIMARY TRIADS. Since all seven tones of a scale are used in the Primary Triads, it is possible to write a melody with them alone. All other triads made on other scale tones are called SECONDARY TRIADS. The Primary Triads are labeled with large Roman numerals. Secondary triads are labeled with small Roman numerals. All Secondary triads from a Major Scale are minor except the one made on the 7th tone. The triad built on the 7th tone is diminished. A small circle is drawn to show that it is diminished: vii°.

EXAMPLE:

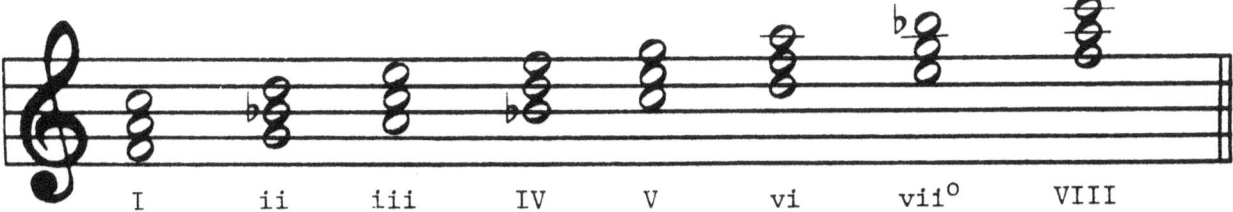

1. Draw Primary Triads from the following scales. Label with Roman numerals. Use accidentals.

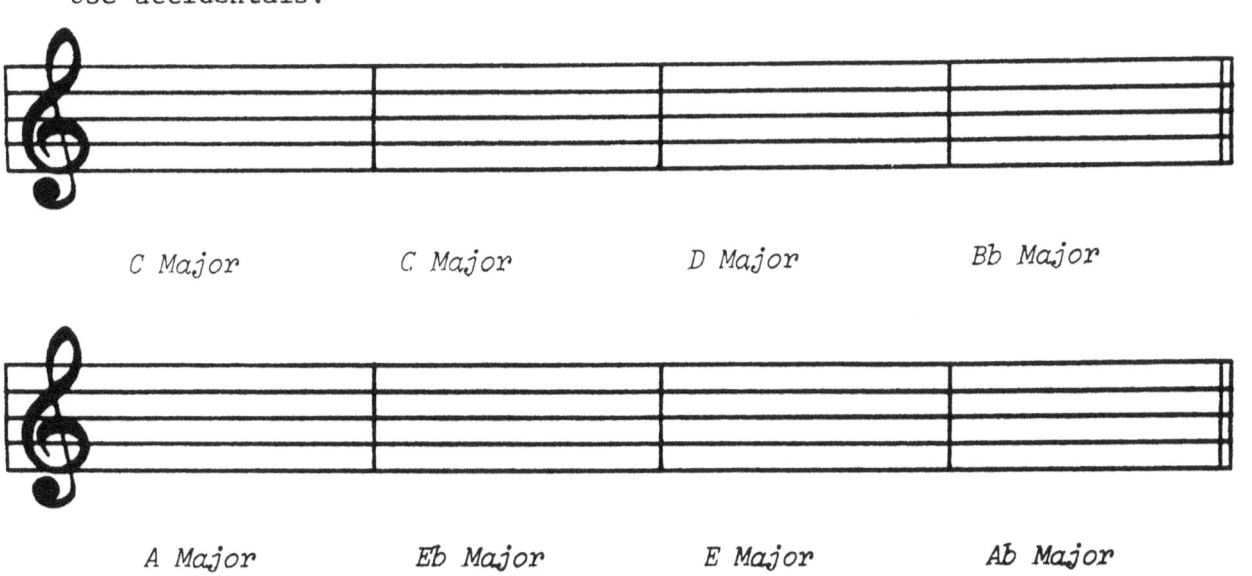

2. Draw secondary triads from the following scales. Label with Roman numerals. Use accidentals.

    C Major   G Major   D Major

    Bb Major   A Major   Eb Major

    E Major   F Major   Ab Major

3. Draw the Natural, Harmonic, and Melodic minor Scales from notes below. Label and use accidentals.

Copy the questions on pages 19 and 20. Write each one in the BASS STAFF. Use manscript paper and add the pages to your notebook.

INVERSIONS OF THE TRIAD

All triads may be played or written in three different positions. When the key-tone is the lowest note of the triad, it is in ROOT POSITION.

ROOT POSITION of a triad:

Notes on three consecutive lines or spaces.

FIRST INVERSION of a triad:

The root is the top note of the triad.

SECOND INVERSION of a triad:

The root is in the middle of the triad.

In each inverted triad there is an interval of a FOURTH. The UPPER NOTE of the fourth is the KEY-TONE of the triad.

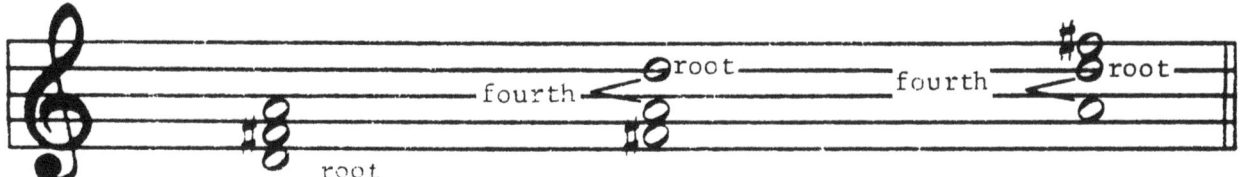

Root Position   1st Inversion   2nd Inversion

REMEMBER: Find the interval of a fourth in any inverted triad - the UPPER NOTE is the KEY-TONE of the triad.

Draw triads and inversions from notes below. Label.

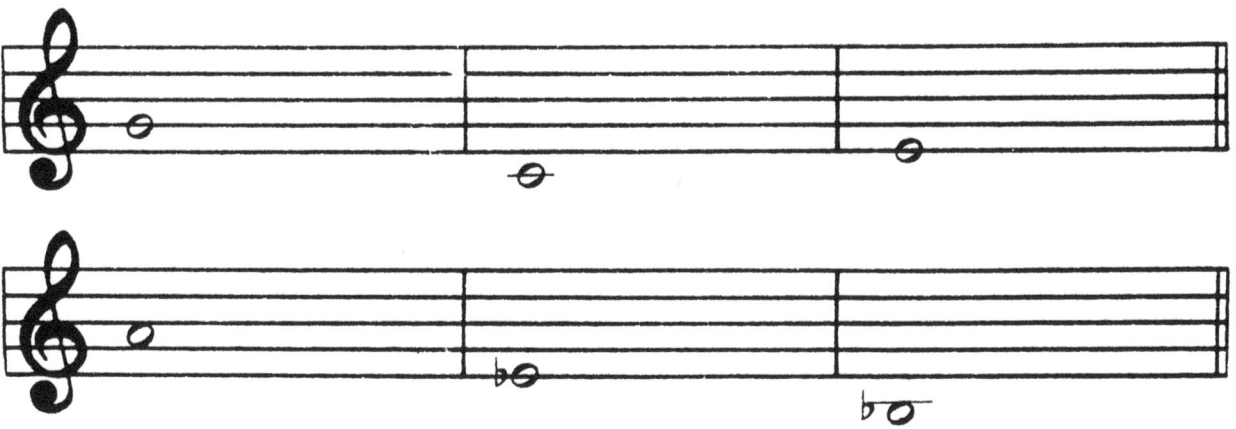

Copyright A46644 by ReSa Publications
CPT 3

WORKSHEET

1. Draw the triads used in Authentic Cadences. Use Key Signatures. Label with Roman numerals.

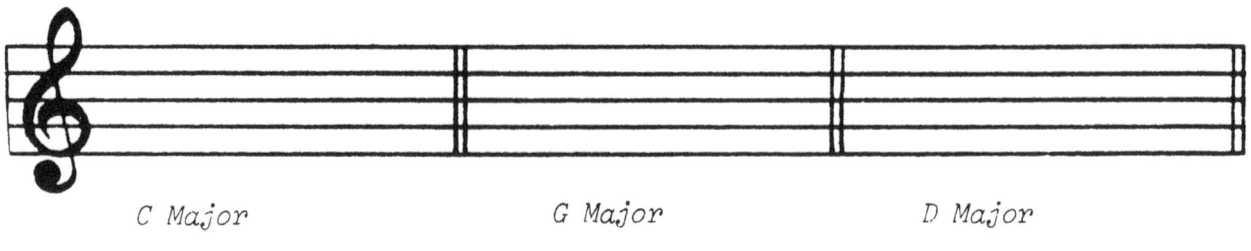

C Major   G Major   D Major

F Major   Bb Major   Eb Major

2. Draw the triads used in Plagal Cadences. Use Key Signatures. Label with Roman numerals.

C Major   G Major   D Major

F Major   Bb Major   Eb Major

DYNAMICS AND TERMS

The Italian words for the following dynamics are:

pp	Pianissimo
p	Piano
mp	Mezzo Piano
mf	Mezzo Forte
f	Forte
ff	Fortissimo

The following Italian terms mean:

Adagio	Slow
Dolce	Sweetly
Lento	Very Slow
Moderato	Medium Tempo
Molto	Much
Poco	A Little
Presto	Very Fast
Vivace	Lively

<u>Motif</u> (Motive) A short figure or phrase used in the development of a composition.

<u>Period</u> An eight, twelve, or sixteen measure musical thought with a cadence at the end.

<u>Phrase</u> Half of a period.

<u>ORNAMENTS</u> (Embellishments)

Grace Note ♪ ♩ A grace note is played before the beat in the Romantic period of music. It is not necessary to the melody line of a composition.

Turn ∾

Trill ∾

Air

Mozart

Andantino

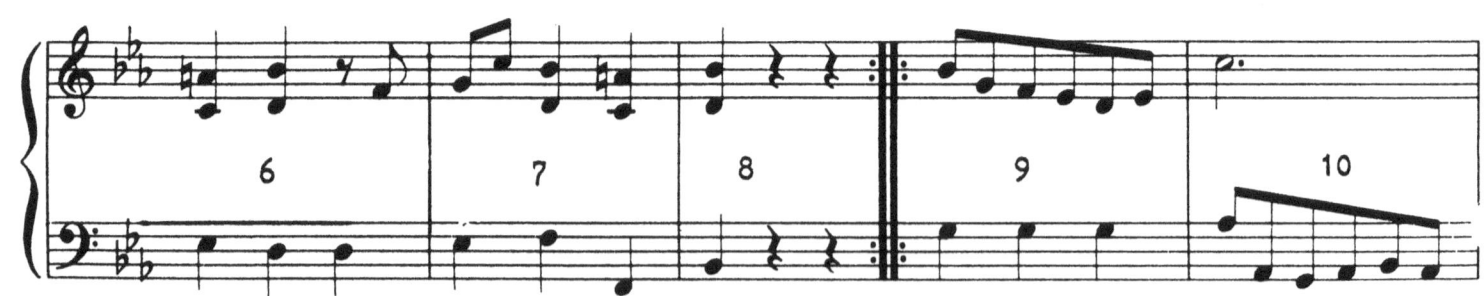

COMPOSITION ANALYSIS

Find the answers to the following questions in the composition on page 24.

1. In what key is the composition written? _____

2. What is the meter? _____

3. What is the tempo? _____

4. In what period of music was it written? _____

5. The cadence between measures 7 and 8 is not in the original key. Write the letter-names that indicate the cadence. (Include both R.H. and L.H. notes.)

   _____ _____ _____   _____ _____ _____

6. What is the key of the cadence? _____

7. Find the following ascending melodic intervals. Write the letter-names of these intervals.

Major 3rd Measure 1 _____ _____	Major 2nd Measure 2 _____ _____
Perfect 4th Measure 3 _____ _____	Perfect octave Measure 11 _____ _____
Perfect octave Measure 13 _____ _____	Perfect 4th Measure 15 _____ _____
Major 2nd Measure 15 _____ _____	

8. Is the cadence between measures 15 and 16 Plagal or Authentic? _____

9. What is the key of the cadence? _____

   Write the letter-names that indicate the cadence.
   (Include both R.H. and L.H. notes.)

   _____ _____ _____   _____ _____ _____

   The tone not shown is _____.

10. Who is the composer of this composition? _____

Copyright A46644 by ReSa Publications
CPT 3

REVIEW TEST

1. Raise each note one half-step. Use an accidental. Do not change the letter-name.

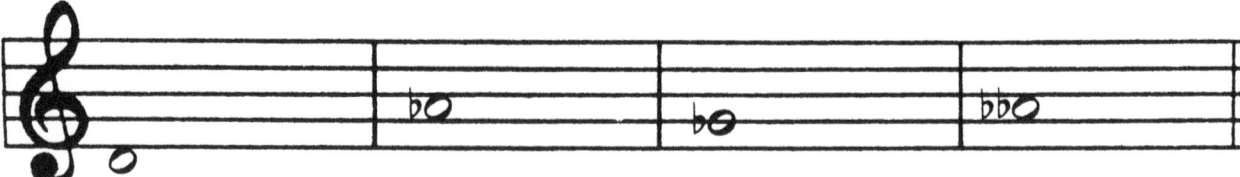

2. Lower each note one whole step. Use an accidental. Do not change the letter-name.

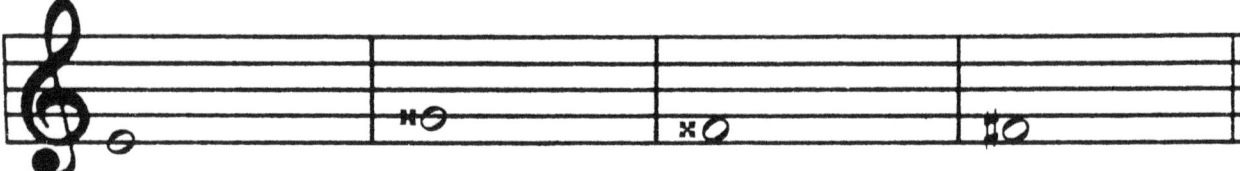

3. Draw the D flat Major Scale one octave. Use accidentals.

4. Draw Major, minor, diminished, and Augmented Triads from notes below. Label.

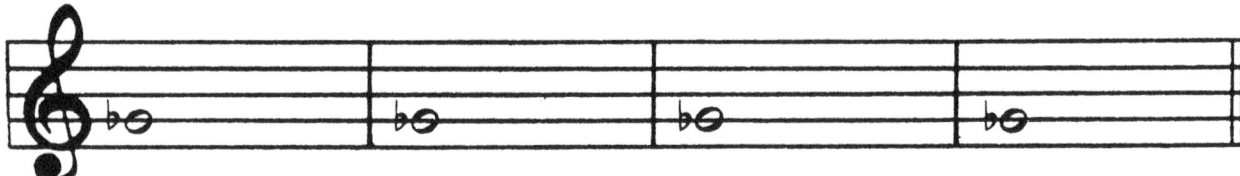

5. Draw the F sharp Major Scale one octave. USE KEY SIGNATURE.

6. Draw Perfect and Major intervals in the key of F Major. Label.

7. Draw Primary Triads in the key of G Major. Use accidentals. Label with Roman numerals.

8. Draw secondary triads in the key of D Major. Use accidentals. Label with Roman numerals.

9. Draw the triads used in a Plagal Cadence and an Authentic Cadence in the key of C Major. Label with Roman numerals.

10. Define the following Italian terms.

Dolce	_____
Vivace	_____
Adagio	_____
Presto	_____
Molto	_____
Allegro	_____
Andante	_____
Moderato	_____
Poco	_____

BAROQUE PERIOD
1600-1750

DOMENICO SCARLATTI   (1685-1757)   Italy

Scarlatti was born in Naples, Italy, during the same year as Handel and Bach. He studied music with his father and became a harpsichord player. A Princess of Portugal studied under Scarlatti before she became the Queen of Spain. During that time Scarlatti lived in Madrid, Spain. He returned to Naples when he was 69. Scarlatti was the foremost composer of keyboard music in the Baroque period. He wrote more than 500 Sonatas for the harpsichord. His compositions are all short and are mainly one-idea pieces in two part form. Even though Scarlatti lived before the piano was invented, he is generally regarded as the father of modern piano playing.

CLASSICAL PERIOD
1750-1820

LUDWIG VAN BEETHOVEN   (1770-1827)   Germany

Beethoven was a composer and performer of tremendous strength and creativity. His father forced him to practice for hours at a time with the desire that his son would make a small fortune for him. He made his debut at the age of eight, but the audience was not very enthusiastic. He lacked that flash of genius with which Mozart had so amazed the world a few years before. He studied under Haydn for a short time, but Haydn was very strict about following the rules of music and Beethoven loved to experiment with harmony and form. He is considered a Classical composer; yet because of this break in tradition, some of his later works are linked to the Romantic period.

His compositions commanded the attention from all who heard them. When he realized he was losing his hearing, he was torn between the desire for life and death. Living was to create music; dying would be better than years without music. His urge to create gave him courage to compose in spite of his deafness.

ROMANTIC PERIOD
1820-1920

FRÉDÉRIC CHOPIN   (1810-1849)   Poland

Chopin was born in a small village near Warsaw, Poland. His father was a professor of French in Warsaw. Chopin heard music played on the piano from the day he was born. At a very early age he begged to take lessons. His sister, only ten years old, was his first teacher. When he was six, he and his sister began to study with Adalbert Zywny. Later his parents placed him under the guidance of Joseph Elsner, with whom he studied composition at the Conservatory of Warsaw. Chopin was considered a genius as a performer. Since he was always in rather delicate health, the concert tours to London in 1848 and 1849 brought on extreme fatigue and hastened his death.

CONTEMPORARY PERIOD
1920-present

DMITRI SHOSTAKOVICH   (1906-1975)   Russia

Shostakovich was born in Leningrad, Russia. His style of composition largely defined the nature of Russian music of that time. His music is popular throughout the world. When he was only five he went to hear an opera with his mother and amazed his family by playing and singing it the next day. His mother gave him his first piano lessons. At the age of thirteen he continued his piano lessons and studied composition at the Leningrad Conservatory. Shostakovich has written many symphonies, operas, compositions for military band and dance band, as well as music for the piano. However, very few of his piano compositions were written for young children. Shostakovich was remarkable because of the unfailing consistency of his style of composition.

Soldiers' March

SCHUMANN

COMPOSITION ANALYSIS

Answers to the following questions are found in the composition on page 30.

1. Write the time values of the notes in measure 1.

   _____   _____   _____

2. Name the circled Harmonic intervals in measure 2.

   _____   _____

3. Name the circled Harmonic intervals in measure 3.

   _____   _____

4. Name the circled Harmonic intervals in measure 4.

   _____   _____

5. Write the time value of the rest in measure 5.

   _____

6. Name the accidental in measure 7.

   _____

7. Name the circled Harmonic intervals in measure 11.

   _____   _____

8. Name the triad in measure 13.

   _____

9. What are the note values in measure 14?

   _____

10. Name the cadence between measures 23 and 24.

    Is it Plagal or Authentic? _____

11. Name the composer of the composition.

    _____

12. In what period of music history was it written?

    _____

RHYTHM AND METER

1. Which number in a Time Signature indicates the meter of the composition?

   (Write Upper or Lower.) _____

2. Write the METER of the following Time Signatures.

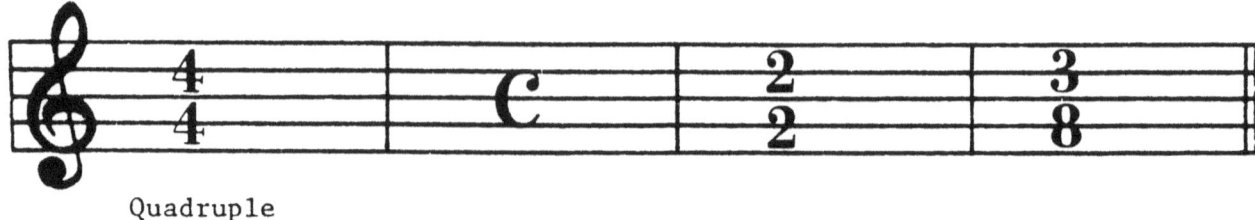

   Quadruple_____   _____   _____   _____

3. Add ONE note that will complete each measure below. Use either ♩ or ♪.
   Write the counting under each measure.

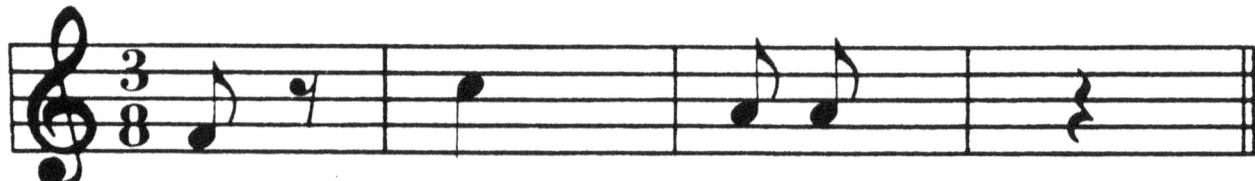

Counts:

Counts:

Counts:

Counts:

WORKSHEET

Name the key of each composition below. One of them has a Plagal
Cadence at the end; the others are Authentic. Name the cadences.

Key of _____   Cadence _____

Key of _____   Cadence _____

Key of _____   Cadence _____

COMPOSITION ANALYSIS

Menuet

Allegretto   Leopold Mozart

Answers to the following questions are found in the above composition.

1. What is the meter of this composition? _____

2. In what key is it written? _____

3. Write the letter-names of the notes on the ledger spaces below the Treble Staff in measure 1.
   _____   _____   _____

4. Name the Harmonic interval in measure 4. _____

5. Name the Harmonic interval in measure 7. _____

6. Write the letter-name of the note on the ledger space below the Bass Staff in measure 9. _____

7. Write the letter-name of the note on the ledger line below the Treble Staff in measure 10. _____

8. Name the note types in measure 12. _____   _____   _____

9. Name the rest in measure 13. _____

10. Is the cadence between measures 15 and 16, Plagal or Authentic? _____

TEST

1. Draw the intervals given below.

   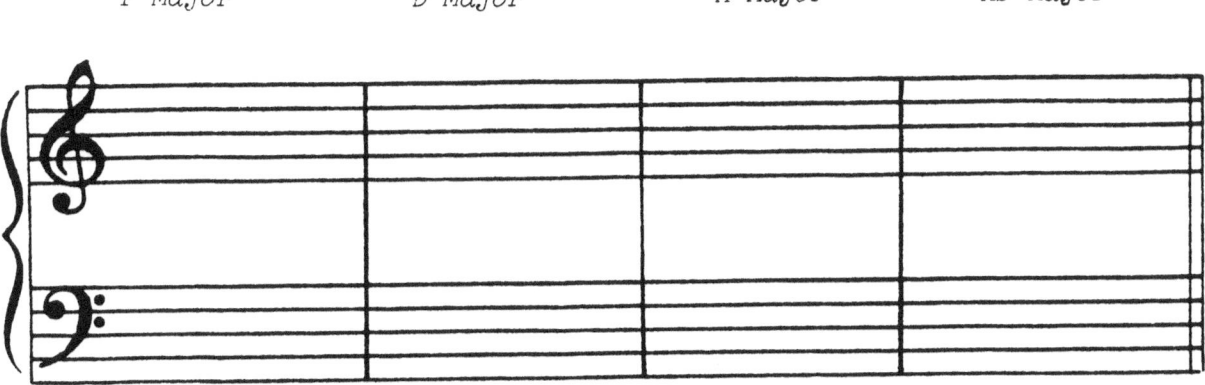

   Perfect 5th   Perfect 4th   Perfect 5th   Perfect 4th

2. Name the following accidentals.

   ♯ _____ ♮ _____ ♭ _____ 𝄪 _____ ♭♭ _____

3. Draw the following notes and rests.

   Quarter-note _____ Half-note _____ Whole note _____

   Quarter-rest _____ Half-rest _____ Whole rest _____

   Eighth-note _____ Eighth-rest _____ Dotted Quarter-note _____

4. Draw a Sixteenth-note triplet. _____

5. Draw the following Key Signatures in both the G Clef and the F Clef.

   F Major   *D Major*   *A Major*   *Ab Major*

6. Draw Major, minor, Augmented, and diminished Triads on notes below. Use accidentals. Label.

6. (continued)

7. Draw PRIMARY TRIADS for the scales of G and D Major. Use accidentals. Label with Roman numerals.

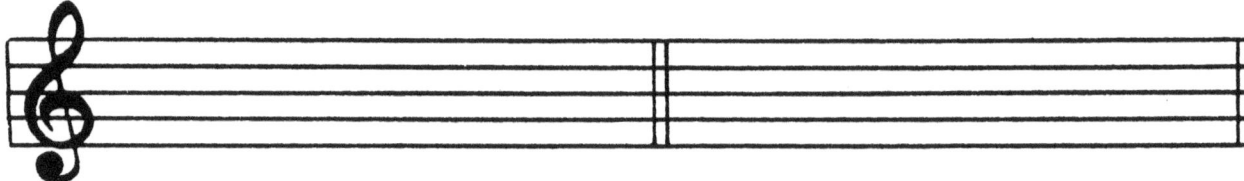

8. Draw SECONDARY TRIADS for the scales of G and D Major. Use accidentals. Label with Roman numerals.

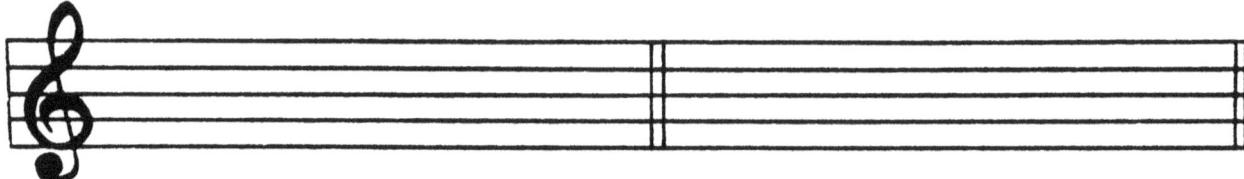

9. Draw the A flat Major Scale one octave. Use accidentals.

10. Name the four periods of music history, a composer from each, and the country where the composer was born.

    _____   _____   _____

    _____   _____   _____

    _____   _____   _____

    _____   _____   _____

11. Draw the triads used in an Authentic Cadence and a Plagal Cadence in the key of F Major. Label with Roman numerals.

12. Give the Italian words for the following.

    *p*_____ *f*_____ *pp*_____ *mp*_____

    *ff*_____ *mf*_____

13. Define the following Italian terms.

    Dolce _____   Moderato _____   Poco _____

    Adagio _____   Presto _____   Vivace _____

    Cresc. _____   Decresc. _____

14. Draw two measures each of duple and triple simple meter.

    DUPLE

    TRIPLE

15. Name three musical instruments.

    _____   _____   _____

16. How many basic melodies are there in ABABA[1]? _____

17. Match the following.

♪♪♪ (triplet)	_____	1. Triple Meter
3/4	_____	2. Secondary Triads
IV V I	_____	3. Moderate Tempo
Moderato	_____	4. Viola
Bach	_____	5. Sixteenth-note
Presto	_____	6. Very Fast
ii iii vi vii°	_____	7. Romantic Composer
♪	_____	8. Duple Simple Meter
Kabalevsky	_____	9. Sixteenth-note Triplet
2/4	_____	10. Tie
𝄾 (eighth rest)	_____	11. Eighth-rest
I IV V	_____	12. Cadence
(tied notes on staff)	_____	13. Modern Composer
String instrument	_____	14. Baroque Composer
Schumann	_____	15. Primary Triads